Waste and R... Colle...

ECO

Published in the United States of America by Cherry Lake Publishing
Ann Arbor, Michigan
www.cherrylakepublishing.com

Reading Adviser: Marla Conn MS, Ed., Literacy specialist, Read-Ability, Inc.
Book Design: Jennifer Wahi
Illustrator: Jeff Bane

Photo Credits: © Rawpixel.com / Shutterstock.com, 5; © Anne Kitzman / Shutterstock.com, 7; © Paul Vasarhelyi / Shutterstock.com, 9; © aldas / Shutterstock.com, 11; © Bernd Schmidt / Shutterstock.com, 13; © kostasgr / Shutterstock.com, 15; © Dmitryp-k / Shutterstock.com, 17; © Stastny_Pavel / Shutterstock.com, 19; © Dmitry Kalinovsky / Shutterstock.com, 21; © Martin Novak / Shutterstock.com, 23; Cover, 2, 3, 8, 10, 20, 24, Jeff Bane

Library of Congress Cataloging-in-Publication Data

Names: Devera, Czeena, author.
Title: Waste and recycling collector / by Czeena Devera.
Description: Ann Arbor : Cherry Lake Publishing, [2018] | Series: My friendly
  neighborhood | Includes index. | Audience: Grades K to 3.
Identifiers: LCCN 2017033512| ISBN 9781534107199 (hardcover) | ISBN
  9781534109179 (PDF) | ISBN 9781534108189 (pbk.) | ISBN 9781534120167
  (hosted ebook)
Subjects: LCSH: Refuse and refuse disposal--Juvenile literature. | Recycling
  (Waste, etc.)--Juvenile literature. | Refuse collectors--Juvenile
  literature.
Classification: LCC TD794 .D48 2018 | DDC 363.72/8--dc23
LC record available at https://lccn.loc.gov/2017033512

Printed in the United States of America
Corporate Graphics

About the author: Czeena Devera grew up in the sweltering heat of Arizona surrounded by books, quite literally as her childhood bedroom had built-in bookshelves constantly overflowing. She now lives in Michigan with an even bigger library of books

About the illustrator: Jeff Bane and his two business partners own a studio along the American River in Folsom, California, home of the 1849 Gold Rush. When Jeff's not sketching or illustrating for clients, he's either swimming or kayaking in the river to relax.

neighborhood helper

People throw out many things. They throw out paper and bottles. These things go into cans. Waste and **recycling collectors** pick up these things.

4

What do you throw out?

Collectors follow a **route**. Some have routes in a neighborhood. Some have routes in a city.

Some drive trucks. The trucks are tall and wide. Some trucks have **robotic arms**. These empty the cans into the trucks.

Who else drives a truck?

Some collectors ride outside the truck. They empty the cans into the truck. They are strong. They are fit.

Collectors follow a **schedule**. They start early. They pick up in the morning.

Collectors pick up in all kinds of weather. They pick up on hot days. They pick up on cold days. They pick up when it rains.

Some collectors pick up waste.
Some pick up the recycling.
Some pick up both.

Collectors empty the truck at a **landfill**. They empty the truck at a recycling place. Some empty the truck at both places.

Collectors stay safe. They wear the right clothes. They wear the right gloves. They wear the right shoes.

Waste and recycling collectors work hard. They keep the neighborhood clean. They keep the city clean.

What would you like to ask a waste and recycling collector?

glossary

collectors (kuh-LEK-turz) people who gather things together

landfill (LAND-fil) a large area where garbage is buried

recycling (ree-SYE-kuhl-ing) old items such as glass, plastic, and newspapers that can be used to make new items

robotic arms (ro-BAH-tic AHRMS) machine arms that work like human arms

route (ROOT) a path that takes someone from one place to the next in an exact order

schedule (SKEJ-ool) a written plan of jobs or activities listed in order by time

index